All profits from this book are being donated to the PEN organisation. PEN is the world's oldest human rights organisation. It aims to promote friendship and intellectual co-operation among writers everywhere; to fight for freedom of expression; and to act as a powerful voice on behalf of writers harassed, imprisoned and sometimes killed for their views.

The Book Mill
www. thebookmill.com

Copyright © of all poems remains with the authors. Individual poems may not be reproduced in any form without the permission of their authors.

Book design and typesetting
by Neil Ferber, The Book Mill

ISBN 978-0-9932045-5-5

The Book Mill is an imprint of
Ferber Jones Ltd
Bongate Mill
Appleby
CA16 6UR

WRITE TO BE COUNTED

Poems to uphold human rights

Edited by
Jacci Bulman,
Nicola Jackson
and Kathleen Jones

The Book Mill

CONTENTS

8 Foreword

11 **Pippa Little** - Against Hate
12 **Maggie Sawkins** - One Fine Morning
13 **Richard J.N Copeland** - The Singularity of the Crowd
14 **Josephine Dickinson** - X is Blue
15 **Pam Zinneman-Hope** -
My Mother Tells Me About Her Washbag,
My Father Tells Me About 1934
About Exile
17 **Mantz Yorke** - Betrayal
18 **Barry Tempest** - To Toussaint L'Ouverture, and all the Others
19 **Allen Ashley** - Casualty of War
20 **Elizabeth Soule** - A Memory of August 1968
21 **Maggie Sawkins** - Elimination
22 **Brigid Rose** - Totalitarian Winter
23 **Martin Rieser** - Icarus
25 **Joan Michelson** - Iranian Woman Judge
26 **Charlie Lambert** - Generation Protest
28 **Simon Cockle** - This is the Post-Truth
29 **Colleen Baran** - Re Search
30 **Agnes Marton** - The Beast Turns Me Into a Tantrumbeast
31 **Christopher Pilling** - A Rich Man in Brittany [trans. Corbiere]
32 **Thomas McColl** - The Full Stop Rebellion
33 **Clare Shaw** - Holding the Line
35 **Emma McGordon** - Queer Beach
37 **Konstandinos Mahoney** - Pride
38 **Carly Brown** - Texas, I Can't Bring You to Parties Anymore
39 **Katherine Gallagher** - Bullies
40 **Josephine Dickinson** - A Deaf Composer at a Computer Music Conference
41 **Hannah Hodgson** - Button Tin
42 **Kathleen Jones** - The Great Dying
43 **Merryn Williams** - Who Now Remembers the Armenians?
44 **Lelia Tanti** - The Journey Home
46 **Martin Rieser** - In Raqqa
47 **Nasrin Parvaz** - Colnbrook Immigration Removal Centre

48 Kenneth Wilson - The Refugees (We miss the smell of almond trees)
49 Lynda Turbet - This is the shoe
51 Charbel Torbey - I . . . a refugee
52 Konstandinos Mahoney - Gift
53 Kerry Darbishire - The Only Road Out is Blocked
54 Carol Caffrey - I Wish I Was Italian
55 Simon Cockle - Together
56 Alison Barr - How Many Smiles?
57 Jacci Bulman - Khanh
58 Sarah Doyle - Unholy
59 Margaret Ives - Bergen-Belsen
60 Danny Rivers - On Golden Beach
61 Ambrose Musiyiwa - The Man Who Ran Through The Tunnel
62 Paul McGrane - Workhouse
63 John Christopher Brown - Steep Stones; Small Steps
64 Ambrose Musiyiwa - Martians. Effing Martians.
65 Charlie Lambert - Statue of Liberty
66 Angela Locke - After the Sky Burial: Tibet
67 Dick Jones - Leon Greenman 1910-2008
    - Migrants
69 Jennifer Johnson - Remembering Srebrenica
70 Sandra Horn - The Day Peace Came
71 Stephanie Green - Give me your Hand
72 Jack Houston - Allinthistogether
74 John Gohorry - You sit on the back row
76 Clare Crossman - Fine Foods est. 1954
77 Kathleen Jones - The Year Zero
78 Sarah Mnatzaganian - Morning
79 Steph Morris - FAQs of Gardens
81 Martyn Halsall - Kavanagh's Field
83 Katherine Gallagher - The Year of the Tree
85 Sarala Estruch - If
86 Carol Caffrey - Post-Partum
87 Alison Luterman - What We Did In The Resistance (Part 1)
89 Christine Vial - Vial Girl
90 Kelly Davis - Georgian Box, Tullie House Museum, Carlisle
91 Lynda Turbet - Spilled Water

92 **Ceinwen Haydon** – No Woman is Indispensable
93 **Elizabeth Stott** - I Grow My Hair
            - Reconstruction
95 **Harriet Fraser** – a sort of hypnosis
97 **Clare Shaw** - Are we there yet?
99 **Mary Powell** - A Weight of Words
101 **Nicola Jackson** - Our Girls
102 **Joan Michelson** - Great Aunt Hero
103 **Pippa Little** - How Helen Steven, Archivist, Scratched an
            Adrienne Rich Poem On Her Cell Door
            in Dumbarton Police Station, Scotland.
104 **Elizabeth Hare** - If Only
106 **Nicola Jackson** - My Wall
107 **Catherine Graham** - Sticks and Stones
108 **Alison Barr** - We Are Clay
110 **Jacci Bulman** - Dancing in Banjul
111 **Chaucer Cameron** - Praise Be to Unexpected Ways
112 **Paul McGrane** - Welcome to my Country

114 **Acknowledgements**

FOREWORD

Nicola Jackson

In June 2016, I was watching an outdoor performance of Midsummer Night's Dream, perched on a bank in drizzly rain. The drama captured the sense of political unreality that began with the referendum result in the UK and intensified through the American election campaign. Horrific events across the globe in the year since, both intentional and accidental, added to my sense that something has changed, that the future of the planet in social and physical terms is genuinely at risk. Never in my generation have values and human rights been more important, and more under threat. This was the stimulus for this anthology. As we spread the word, we found likeminds right across a spectrum of poets, and a sense of community from Lebanon to Cambodia and across Europe. We hope that making our case for the right of every human being to have a valid and positive life, within a global community that is responsible to our planet, may extend that fellowship and help us all look positively to the new future.

Jacci Bulman

Why do I believe in the power of this anthology to uphold human rights? I read recently of a woman from the minority 'Yazidi' religion, who was captured in northern Iraq, and repeatedly sold on the slave market (mostly for sex) by ISIS terrorists. She was rescued by one of her people and the leader of her religion made a brave decision to change their strict, traditional rules, (excluding anyone who had sex outside their faith, even by rape) and welcome women who have suffered like her back in, with ritual blessings. This was an act of hope. To rise up to a better, more understanding future. Because love helps us do that: to fill dark voids of fear and exclusion with new acceptance and light. I believe that these poems are full of that light, and will help us all to rise up and genuinely make our world for the many, not the few. I believe these are poems of hope.

Kathleen Jones

Editing this anthology has been a humbling, challenging and ultimately uplifting task. Like my co-editors I was filled with sadness and despair as I watched world events unfold, feeling impotent to change anything. But to know that so many other people also feel like this and are willing to step forward 'to be counted' is inspirational. We have to stand up for human rights, and this includes the right to live on a planet that is fit for habitation. The environment is in crisis. What can I do as a writer? As Pippa Little says in her poem 'Against Hate', *'This is my act, to write,'* because *'today is bloody, inexplicable'*. All the poets in this anthology have put words on paper in order to be counted. On our own we can do very little. Together, we can make ourselves heard.

"All human beings are born free and equal in dignity and rights."
　　Universal Declaration of Human Rights, (1948) Article 1

"For to be free is not merely to cast off one's chains, but to live in a way that respects and enhances the freedom of others."
　　Nelson Mandela

Pippa Little

Against Hate

Sole passenger on an early morning tram
I'm half asleep when the driver brakes,
dashes past me, dives into a copse of trees,
gone for so long I almost get out to walk.
Then he's back, his face alight.
I saw the wren! Explaining
how he feeds her when he can
and her restless, secretive waiting.
We talk of things we love until the station.

I tell him of the Budapest to Moscow train
brought to a halt in the middle of nowhere,
everyone leaning out expecting calamity
but not the engine driver, an old man
kneeling to gather armfuls of wild lilies,
wild orchids. He carried them back
as you would a newborn, top-heavy, gangly,
supporting the frail stems in his big, shovel hands.
These are small things, but I pass them on

because today is bloody, inexplicable
and this is my act, to write,
to feel the light against my back.

Maggie Sawkins

One Fine Morning
With thoughts of Jean Charles de Menezes 7.01.78 – 22.07.05)

And it could have been ours –
the heart skipping out of bed
one fine morning.

The heart with the day singing in its ears,
reaching for its coat,
closing the door.

And it could have been ours –
the heart finding itself caught
with its toes on the starting line,
tricked into running
over fields, over fences, over stiles.

And it could have been ours –
the heart tripping over itself,
its face to the land,
deafened by its own hooves of thunder.

And it could have been ours –
the heart both less and more
than a grain of sand –
without doing anything wrong,
the heart struck dumb, like a dog's,
one fine morning

Richard J. N. Copeland

The Singularity of the Crowd

No part of this. I want no part
in the popular flow of
> *we are one, and*
> *we speak with a single voice*
> *to solidify our unity against*
> *the other's oneness.*

Not that at all. Dare I then sing of the man who said no;
the one who turned his back and said
I will not kiss your fucking flag?*

Thus against the trend he stood
as the crowd rose to condemn the dissenter

> *for we are one and*
> *we speak with a single voice*

or so they claimed, but at the time
not all thought the same, yet did not dare
utter except to say hello

> as was the custom
> of the crowd
> for as a mass
> they spoke as one.
> They said so,
>   thought   ditto.

So let us consider the one who stands
defiant against the state, the unit grown
to more than an individual
> one, he, she, you

> or   me.

*ref: e. e. cummings

Josephine Dickinson

X is Blue

X is blue. True X is not blue.
My feeling is that blue obliterates yellow.
I didn't see why she would be seen
with him. After all, X is not blue.
True X is blue. False X is blue.
I have weak arms, I have pimples.
X is yellow. False X is blue.
True, I have pimples but she didn't seem to notice
and therefore like or not like everything about them.
X is yellow. True X is not blue.
True X is not what it is in their past
that's making them like or not like
yellow. True X is not blue.

Pam Zinnemann-Hope

My Mother Tells Me About Her Washbag

Kiev Prison 1937

We have to cross
a cold stone courtyard
with our washbags;
we have to walk naked
while male guards
watch us.
I feel covered in bedbugs.

My Father Tells Me About 1934

I'm working in the Jewish Hospital now,
walk out onto the street;
someone comes up to me rattling a tin
collecting for the Nazis.

I tell her, you should be ashamed of yourself,
collecting for such a cause.

From out of my words, around a corner
four SS appear, to arrest me.

I feel a pause; a crowd of ordinary
Frankfurt people form around me,
move forward spontaneously,
push me into a tram.

Father, do you hate the Germans?

I owe my life to them.

Pam Zinnemann-Hope

About Exile

Where before there was an openness,
suddenly her brown eyes are impenetrable.
She talks about her own country;
the hot dusty place where she began her life,
fresh pomegranates, the harbour;
when she touches on the living texture of marble and bees,
I see the shutters go up at the windows of her old house.

And I know the stone her clear song springs from.

Mantz Yorke

Betrayal

What loyalty made you leak material
declared classified or inappropriate
for all to know? Security necessitates
some silence, but what morality conceals

diplomacy sweetening deals with bribes,
contractors abusing human rights,
random shootings in a fury of revenge,
families blasted by misdirected bombs?

Your treatment on remand – *cruel and unusual*,
denied exercise, light, and sometimes clothes –
and a sentence as lengthy as a murderer's
suggests the Eighth Amendment no longer holds.*

Your match lit up dark closets of the state,
but who is the betrayer; who is the betrayed?

*The Eighth Amendment to the US Constitution prohibits the federal government from imposing, inter alia, cruel and unusual punishments, including torture.

Barry Tempest

To Toussaint L'Ouverture, and all the Others

Most unhappy man of men! Wordsworth wrote
to give support to one who tried and failed;
found hope in *breathing of the common wind*,
placed trust in *man's unconquerable mind*.

Move on a little way. Before the notes
were fully scored, the dedication inked
on Beethoven's *Sinfonia Eroica*,
the purposed honouring was torn, decayed,

the memory drifting through thick battle-smoke:
the *grand'uomo* pinned an empire to his coat.
Fidelio's trumpet that Napoleon betrayed
broke down a dungeon wall, renewed the wind

that Wordsworth blew from Toussaint's festering cell:
the wind still blows, scattering uranium dust
on orange jump-suits, water-boarding blocks,
but still there is that trumpet, far off, just.

Allen Ashley

Casualty of War

'In war, truth is the first casualty.'
Aeschylus, (525 BC - 456 BC)

Truth is the first casualty of war;
closely followed by her brother, Honesty.
It's not long until their cousins
Decency, Fair Play and Do the Right Thing
are also mown down by
the machine guns.
An air strike takes out the
gutsy rebellion of Hold Fast To Your
Core Values;
unmanned drones obliterate the
Moral High Ground.
Not to be outdone, our battleships
have pulverised the seaport of
Help Your Fellow Man;
whilst the enemy's navy has retaliated by blowing the
sacred island of Altruism
clean out of the water.
Objectivity maintains a few remaining
strongholds
but she is surrounded, doomed.
A new family of values is moving in:
Certainty, Zeal, Unquestioning Faith, Expediency and
the Mr Fix-it of our times –
Getting The Job Done.
Why do you still resist?

Elizabeth Soule

A Memory of August 1968
For Vaclav Havel, d. 18th December 2011

In a starless chill before dawn
we stood by the water's edge,
tiny points of candle-light.
A solitary flute sang out our misery
to the vastness of a dark sea.

Some had crouched over the radio all night
and guessing the worst,
had woken us
to stumble from tents to our hopeless vigil,
while hundreds of miles away
another darkness rumbled over the frontier,
grinding the dreams of Spring
beneath remorseless tracks.

Then in bitter, barren silence
one by one each candle was extinguished,
our futile tribute
to those who dared to dream.

But hope and freedom are seeds that will not sleep
and the dust of dreams is fertile ground.
Small bright shoots split stone,
shatter concrete,
their progress more inexorable
than any trundling tank.

The brave gardener whose fearless tending
of improbable seedlings
gave us back belief,
now returns himself to the nurturing earth
and reminds us
that when the darkness seems most complete,
dawn is not so far away.

Maggie Sawkins

Elimination

Although he came from the mountains
(this much I learnt)

he didn't understand my words
for snow.

I fluttered my fingers
in front of him

but he only saw
the wings of birds.

I led him to the window
wrapped myself in my arms

at the shivering sky
but he only stared.

It was slow and involved
the elimination

of sun, wind and rain
but we got there.

Sometimes I think of him
back at the border

I imagine his mountains
their fingers of shadow

the stutter of gunfire
the quietness of snow.

Brigid Rose

Totalitarian Winter

The snow came overnight like an army trained in perfect stealth
and silent manoeuvres bringing in its new white regime.
What was once familiar and ordinary became transposed
into something brave and unexplained that we were too awed to question.
In the morning looking out, we viewed The New World.
Everything was clear and gleaming.
With better eyes we saw what dignity the fields had.
The streets were noble and dangerous.
The banners and slogans that hung along fences and telegraph wires –
how could we not believe in them?

We walked out, wary where we trod,
saw each individual twig and blade defined to precision,
saw the weary arms of trees subdued by a brilliance unblemished,
saw ice form swords of truth, weapons where once
there was only water.
How hushed and peaceful everything seemed.
When we spoke out across snow a muffling occurred.
Our words hit white and were silenced.

And the ice remains, holds tight, freezes harder still.
It's a season that was planned to last.
But we are uniformly glad
that answers can be simpler now in this world of white and black.

Martin Rieser

Icarus
*For Jacques Marie Charles Trolley Prévaux:
Born 2 April, 1888, Died 19 August, 1944*

1919

What lives, drags itself
back to the ruined towns,
moving like trackless ants
over rubble and torn earth.

From the cockpit
I can see trenches
and shatterings,
all the tiny paraphernalia
of death.

I wind the camera.
The plane's shadow bubbles
over the front's pocked
and futile corridor.

1944

In the Marseille dazzle,
they came for us
dressed in stifling black.
I stared hard at the sun.

In Monluc there is no light
except the torturer's electric spark.
I climb through clouds of pain
to blue silence.

If I could only go higher
I would see the curve

of this small planet
and the light of stars.

With the scent of burnt flesh,
of feathers: I am ready
now for the long
wingless fall into silence.

Joan Michelson

Iranian Woman Judge

Defending human rights, I stayed.
Stayed while I was watched.
Stayed through threats to end my life.
Stayed for nearly thirty years.
I did not know a life alone.
This life without a home.
The driver parked outside my house.
Was I forgetting something?
My husband waited by the door.
He held my mother's Koran high.
I passed beneath it back and forth,
back and forth, back and forth.
Then I bent to kiss the cover.
My husband squeezed my arm.
If I had known. If he had known.
He said so easily, 'Come back quickly.'

Charlie Lambert

Generation Protest

Who'd have thought in '71
When Marvin asked
What's going on?

Who in '64 stayed dumb
When Sam Cooke said
That *change will come?*

Who denied the human plea
When Nina wished
Just *to be free?*

Jamaica heard the voice of reason
When Marley wrote
Those songs of freedom

And Fela Kuti's Afro beats
Put question marks
On Lagos streets.

Paul Simon wrote a song back then
Of churches burnt
By hooded men

And Lennon shared his great romance:
Lie back in bed,
Give peace a chance.

Joan Baez had the right idea:
Woodstock days, but
Did we hear?

Fifty years, and have we binned
Dylan
Blowin' in the wind?

Joni got it right it seems.
Chance of peace
Was *just our dreams*.

But were we wrong to march and sing,
Scatter flowers, bang the drum?
Or can we promise even now
The day when *we shall overcome*?

Simon Cockle

This is the Post-Truth

This is a fact, not a lie;
the words are familiar,
the syntax soothing
though the meaning may jar.

This is a fence, not a wall;
keeping in goodness,
marking the boundary
between them and us.

This is a hand, not a fist;
don't be fooled
by the curl and clench,
the knuckles' whiteness.

This is a wand, not a gun;
see this trick we perform
while the muzzle rests,
like magic, at your temple.

This is a ladder, not a noose;
a hoop for a step,
a rope to clutch at
that lifts you to heaven.

Colleen Baran

Re Search

as 1984 tops the bestseller list
alternative facts are the new
fake news

resist, insist, persist

as google searches for
the definition of "fact" trend

searches for facts
trend

search
re
search
research

or

doublespeak
doublethink
don't think

as newspaper headlines
rouse one
to weigh the difference between an untruth, a falsehood, and a lie

like the many northern words for snow and ice

reading

how to navigate the landscape
traversing the new terrain

Agnes Marton

The Beast Turns Me Into a Tantrumbeast

You are me (said the beast).

From now on
I'm your nameless shelter.

Fear my dreams
half-awake, run.

Ripe in my poison
like cherries,
chase my ways.

Don't pray, dissolve
in my summer breath.

Our limbs are
overlapping meadows,
hazy honey landscape.

By myself (I told the beast).
Teeth away or I squeak.
Mellific, knotty bully
stepping on all that I bear.
Don't push me under your reign.
Who do you think you are.
Leave me alone, I build my own.
I fear my own, I dream my own.

Beastie, come on.

Chris Pilling

A Rich Man in Brittany*

> *O fortunatos nimium, sua si* . . .
>   Virgil

He's rich, this Breton hobo, who is poor and old,
Yes, and homeless, unwashed, lousy, with not far to fall!
– He's a philosopher-errant of the open road,
Partial to dry black bread – not buttered with gall . . .
If there is none: good-night. – He knows of a manger
Where the cow loans a little fresh straw to the stranger;
There he'll fall asleep, dream of feasting at the bread-board,
And wake up in the morning, agape at the Good Lord
– *Panem nostrum* . . . – His hunger has the savour of hope . . .
A belly *Benedicite* is given full scope;
Well he knows that the eye above is never shut,
In its twinkling there fell manna in the desert
And the bread in his pouch . . .
                    From farm to farm he goes.
At the sound of his step there are no doors that close,
– For his coming's propitious. – In he comes and,
Having lighted his pipe by blowing on a firebrand,
Sits down. – When there's food to spare folk are generous;
So he bestirs himself and laughs, coughs and chunners
A *pater* in Hebrew. Then, taking up his cane
With an: I'll be back – he's off on his rounds again.
The huge dog in the yard rubs up against his leg . . .
– With nuzzling like that, do you really need your Meg? . . .
And – who knows — in the fields, one fine day, an empress
May let her hair down too and distribute largesse . . .

[* Extract. Translated from the original French of Tristan Corbiere]

Thomas McColl

The Full Stop Rebellion

Full stops will go on strike from 9pm on Monday night
in protest at being constantly forced
to prop up dictatorial statements
and provide their round signatures
to half-truths and outright lies.

This strike will affect both speech and print.
Commas can't be relied upon – some may strike in support.

The public should refrain from non-essential
speaking, writing, typing and reading.
There is the real possibility of death
from not being able to pause for breath.

The chattering classes have been warned
that the choice could be as stark as shut up or die.
Hospitals are on standby.
Emergency wards have this week
been stocked with large consignments
of compliant full stops, imported from Qatar,
for use in life saving sentences
(It's believed that Britain's 'good friend' in the Gulf
will get a dozen new tanks by way of thanks
for stepping in so quickly with supplies).

News just in:
The Government is rushing through a new law
to elevate the status of the colon.

"It makes perfect sense," insists the Prime Minister.
"Two dots are clearly more of a full stop than one dot."

No-one knows yet though if demotion of the full stop
will avert the looming crisis...

Clare Shaw

Holding the Line

To refuse to change one's practice or plans.
I was holding the hand of a stranger
in Manchester. It was late June,
early evening, there were thousands
of us. I was holding the line with drag queens;
leathermen; a young Russian who was visiting friends.

To hold the melody, to remain steady
For years I was too scared to sing
but last night, we were twenty on stage.
Maybe you are that blonde woman
who smiled like a laugh about to happen.
It took me some time to come home

A military tactic, in which a line of troops
is supposed to prevent an enemy breakthrough
but now I know who I am and I know my people
there were thousands of us, the line extending
round Velvet, the New Union, Paddy's Goose
till the Village was circled completely and maybe

you are the dark-haired woman who punched the air,
or perhaps you stood at the back *To keep a phone line open*
and I did not catch your eye. I remembered
how good it is to be conducted, to watch someone's hands
like a language; to be told when to start
and stop. *To firmly maintain one's view.*

We rewrote the line we were given,
we will not walk it. We were all facing out;
into the city and straight into the cameras,
people calling from buses. I was holding the hand
of a young man from Russia, I was holding
my daughter's hand. *To not yield to the pressure*

of a difficult situation. They will not pass. We will not let them
we cannot stop them. They cannot stop us
from singing and holding hands. Does your hand in mine
feel shy like a creature? We are taking the stage.
Are you from Russia? It took me some time to find you.
It took me some time to come home.

Emma McGordon

Queer Beach.

On the beach, back against a rock,
watched a man and his son, maybe four, five, and six dogs.

I knew his type, heard on the wind the crack
about getting sweets from the 'Paki shop.'

Maybe I hunched a bit harder, stared further to sea as the sound
of his boots packing the stones grew louder.

When he says - "Alright, Bud?" cocking his chin to the side, making his
 cigarette falter,
I feel his mistake, and I wonder, if he'd known, would he have bothered to speak.

A woman alone on the beach as the tide was turning
the sun going down among clouds.

I didn't flinch when the dogs came closer, sniffed my neck like a whisper,
noses crusted with sand and salt on their whiskers.

"Leave him", he shouts, a lad grown up round here used to lurchers and
lamping, the skinning of rabbits at dawn.

It's happened before, I've been a that or an it,
a hybrid match of mixed-up bits.

When he's left, I walk back along the cliffs,
red sandstone, green gorse that's just beginning to bud yellow.

I spy rabbits that seem to care about nothing
but the not being seen.

A woman with her dog in the distance frowns an expression like
her lips could be the tight clasps that will keep me from mugging
 her, or worse.

It's dusk and I get it; the clothes, the walk, the hood
but I see the leather of her face soften when she realises

this isn't a boy alone at dusk about to fork through her path
and I wish, that when that man with his son said "alright bud,"

I hadn't hunched my shoulders more, I wish I hadn't replied
"alright pal", in a voice as a low as mine would go,

but most of all, I wish that I'd been wrong, wish he'd known all along
I was a woman on a beach, back against a rock, staring out to sea

and for him to say Alright bud, and walk on
was just the way it was.

Konstandinos Mahoney

Pride

And the trans woman in the gold lurex leotard
is sparkling in the sun as she pushes her bike before us,
pup boys, eyes glittering behind dog hoods,
strain ahead on leather leashes and, as we round the corner,
a breeze catches our flag and the crowds lined up on either side
the length of Oxford Street cheer, and I hold your hand,
man and man, as we march fearless to Trafalgar Square.

Parade over, marshals wave us to a side road.
We stack banners, furl flags, group photos on our phones,
trans woman cycles home, pup boys trot off with their handlers
and, as we walk to the station, merging back into the crowd,
tourists, shoppers, locals, people out to drink, eat, have fun,
the sun is curtained by a cloud and we're no longer holding hands.

Carly Brown

Texas, I Can't Bring You to Parties Anymore [Extract*]

Texas, I find you
passed out
drunk
in front of the neighbor's lawn, clutching
a Taser gun because you shot the family's
golden retriever Trixie,
insisting she was rabid
and resisting citizen's arrest.

Texas,
is this some kind of test
you are putting me through?
To see how much I love you
by doing
    every
        stupid thing
        you can think of to do?

Then bringing me here
to wipe off your sallow cheeks lined
with sticky oil crying and dehydration,
asking me to take you back
inside to face my friends
and an entire nation
        waiting

for some sort of apology.

*the whole poem can be viewed on this link
https://www.youtube.com/watch?v=JOJKaZIHqGI/

Katherine Gallagher

Bullies

With the eye in the back of his head
he sees them coming

eight-year-old breakers,
baby-hard, baby-soft.

Their elegant space-machine
could swallow him,

drown him once and for all
in a dish of air.

He freezes
as they expect

though a voice inside him squeaks I...
Words cut his tongue,

weigh in his mind
like a bruise.

Josephine Dickinson

A Deaf Composer at a Computer Music Conference

Have you any English papers, books?
Map, but in fact, the point is, the problem is
imagining how it would affect
experience in a childhood. Quote
the experience. We can but play it new.

Is this the .... memorial?
Don't know. Now the big thing
to think language, tape real time,
play time and check time as a musician.
The doom of poet are simply the doom
of processes. Any more conversation?

Some of the things need mending.
Many the doom of poet. So on.
Any more conversation? Now erm
just maybe complete what I'm saying to you.
Ten questions. Fold and rotate guitar D.
Perfect undersound. As I said I don't know.

I don't feel well. Turbulence.
Main factor is, because of this
that is rich and source of energy.
This is such a sleepy .... after that, OK,
conversation confiscated the funeral.
We can but play it new.

Be very careful with these things.
Why does one hit a drum or anything?
We compose that growl in two distinct forms.
Phoomf phoomf purr!
doomf purr!! doomf.
Good. Thank you.

Hannah Hodgson

Button Tin

Bagged, the spare buttons
that are tagged to clothing –
the same, just as capable

just unemployed,
missing a stitch.
We don't call buttons

scroungers of the tin.
Don't shame them, just wait
for a vacancy.

Jobless buttons aren't shamed –
so why treat unemployed humans
so harshly?

Kathleen Jones

The Great Dying

For those whose bones
lie only an inch under the grass
I have only words.
Below the skin of moss or turf
they lie where they were felled
in hundreds
where the trees are greenest.

There are places yet to find
where the teeth of ancestors
still speak to us from the forest floor
among the foxgloves and pine needles
and sapling spruce. Or woven among
the roots of a hundred year old hemlock
downed in the last El Nino wind.

And sometimes the storms
will show a father
teaching his son the old places,
a cave stacked with
cedar boxes and a shaman's staff wedged
between stones in the roof.

The laughing picnickers,
whose yacht is moored offshore,
know nothing of a genocide;
the baby suckling at a rotting breast
the grandparents too weak to gather food
the girl abandoned out of fear.

The mortuary stench that kept the ships
from shore has long since vanished
but the bones
like human cruelty
are more firmly rooted.

Merryn Williams

Who Now Remembers the Armenians?

Who now remembers the Armenians?
There are mass graves and illegible stones.

Snow falls on an unending plain,
skies blur, the tape winds back again.

And there will always be a man
Who will smilingly lift the telephone,

'the names you want are at this address,
can I have the reward, please?'

Our lips are numbed by all that snow,
where are the voices that say no?

Ruanda, Chechnya, Armenia,

the names grow faint,

remember
                        remember

Lelia Tanti

The Journey Home

Built with the pieces
of a half-remembered song in another language,
its words a lonely secret,
I sing it to myself sometimes, knowing
the journey home is make-believe.

Each day the end of it pushed further
as time and distance muddle what had once been clear,
the voice still cries out. When?
My journey home gets longer.

The foreign spotlight shines brightest from within
threatening to blow my cover –
I must declare myself at customs.
In the house of the dislodged,
morsels feed a habit of remembrance.
The bread I taste breaks open a familiar hunger,
delivers me, once more,
to the uncharted course that will be always
the same journey home. The trail
of crumbs I left now gone, both shelter and burden
are the memories locked in my clenched fist.

Oh, if the bones of buildings
bare and naked, foundations exposed
and left to gather moss,
if only they (who know what it is to be unfinished)
could offer solace, because

the journey home will kick
like an animal in fright just
as I think I have it tamed.
Thirsty, taking more than it gives,
wanting payment
with my sleep, whispering

its half-demented yearnings
in the dark –
the endless loop, the endless loop,
the crazy talk.

Martin Rieser

In Raqqa

For Ruqia Hassan 1985-2015

If we pay attention to the soldered sky
it is spliced to the earth by imaginary ladders.
No one has shown us any love, except the graveyards.
No one has shown any compassion, except the graveyards.

If we pay attention to the staggered roofs
the music of smoke writes itself randomly.
End this darkness, these random acts of dislocation:
crucifixion in the squares, whippings on the corners.

If we pay attention to the street, metal rains down,
fire rains down, rubble falls and the jets pass.
Walls are painted black, blackness covers our heads,
even our hands are covered. Without dignity life is worthless.

If we pay attention to their voices, they sound like thorns
and our truth spills red onto the ground.
My soul is free, but my body theirs to break as they will.
We shall not bend, but we will die tomorrow or today.

Nasrin Parvaz

Colnbrook Immigration Removal Centre

You wake up to the sound of
the first early morning plane
landing at Heathrow.
Then you go back to your dreams
thinking about the passengers in the plane
wondering if any of them are like you.
Traveling on a false passport.

Hazily you remember
that some rich man
has bought this prison
all the inmates included
just like serfs or slaves
and you try to figure out
how anyone makes money
holding you prisoner.

Kenneth Wilson

The Refugees
(We miss the smell of almond trees)

We miss the smell of almond trees,
And Hafiz read on lovers' seat;
We miss the dawn-warmed desert's breeze.

We miss the chew of charred sheep's cheese,
The market's steaming beetroots' heat.
We miss the smell of almond trees,

The blue-tiled mosque, the sweet tea's ease,
Spiced nights of hot un-measured meat.
We miss the dawn-warmed desert's breeze.

And now – at borders strangers seize
Us roughly, scorn us our defeat,
Far from the smell of almond trees.

Countries crossed at winter's freeze,
Backs bent, and slow on bloodied feet;
We miss the dawn-warmed desert's breeze.

We miss those tiny earth-grimed knees,
Our children laid out on the street,
Their souls now dawn-warmed desert's breeze.
Oh, God, the smell of almond trees.

Lynda Turbet

This is the shoe

This is the shoe that was found on the beach at Lesbos.

This is the child who wore the shoe
that's buried in sand on Lesbos.

This is the boat that sank with the child
the father and mother the sister and brother
beneath the waves of Lesbos.

This is the trafficker ruthless and cold
who hired the boat the leaking boat
(that carried the child who wore the shoe)
that sank off the coast of Lesbos.

This is the man who swam to the shore
to rescue the child the terrified child
who sank with the boat the trafficker hired
who wore the shoe
that lay on the beach at Lesbos.

This is a tent the home of the man
the traumatised man escaping from war
who rescued the child who sank with the boat
the father and mother the sister and brother,
who paid the trafficker greedy and cold
to take them safely to Lesbos.

This is the country that sent a tent
but closed its door on the traumatised man
who fled the bombs who swam to the shore
to save the child who lost the shoe
that hides in the sand on Lesbos.

This is the voter who said 'No more'
who lives in the country that sent the tent

but closed its door
on the desperate man who fled from war
who paid the trafficker thousands of pounds
for a place on the boat the ancient boat,
that over-turned in the pitching sea
who rescued the child who lost the shoe
that rots on the beach at Lesbos.

Charbel Torbey

I ... a refugee.

How did I finish here?
Salty water hurts
Wounds of war...
Of despair and wander!
Is there a future?
Welcoming soils... distant lands.
I'm lost as ever before.
The jungle is human!
Everywhere the same story.
What to say and tell?
The story is the same...
The headlines are the same...
The cold is the same...
Shake hands, forget tomorrow!
Now is a dream... a nightmare of beasts.
Here I stand,
Like a wounded *torero*...
An arena of eyes.
Curious to see, never to listen.
Like an autumn leaf,
I fall.
I ... a refugee.
With a Rosa Damascena in my hand...

Konstandinos Mahoney

Gift

If you see us climbing over the wall
into your garden,
do not call the police,
we come with gifts,
not in these ragged bundles,
no frankincense or myrrh in there,
no gold hidden in the lining.

We bring you something else,
something mislaid for so long
you have forgotten what it was.
As you open the door to let us in,
perhaps you will remember
what it was you once lost,
for now it is found.

Kerry Darbishire

The Only Road Out is Blocked

Somewhere someone like me has just died.
I watch the news and cry.
During the adverts I put the kettle on.
Owls are setting up in sycamore branches
silhouetted against an almost full moon.
Upstairs my children are still not going to sleep –
it no longer matters.
Someone like me can't hear their children
bleeding short lives away under rubble
and dust. Not moving. Not playing catch
not dreaming in a bedroom now crushed
to the size of a coffin.
He's telling us ...*targeting civilian areas continues
and the only road out is blocked*...
What can I do?
All they have left seeps from their eyes.
I try to imagine everyone I know and love
has disappeared, that the past meant nothing
and the future has drained to an ugly shade of red.
I'm too safe, too warm tonight – making plans,
reading poetry, letting in the cat while someone
somewhere is fighting for air, drowned, scared
of the clouded street they no longer recognise,
carrying a rusty tin to find food, water, anything.
In the time it takes me to make tea, the moon
has gone searching for a city it once knew.

Carol Caffrey

I Wish I Was Italian

I wish I was Italian.
Formaggio, adagio and *grigio*
sound much more lovely than
cheese, slowly, grey,
don't they?

Simon Cockle

Together

> *"You've got a swarm of people coming across the Mediterranean seeking a better life, wanting to come to Britain."* David Cameron

these are our faces
regarding each lorry
like an iron ark, moving
across the tarmac waves
together

these are our hands
gripping the wire fence
as if pulling the coastlines
still closer and closer
together

these are our mouths
calling out the place names
and sounds of our home towns
where families wait for news
together

these are our feet
worn down with running
from beaches to borders
or standing in lines
together

this is your swarm, then;
sharing the burden
of displacement,
the search for a better life
together

Alison Barr

How many Smiles?

Push the curled-up child
wearing a red T-shirt,
black shorts, best shoes.
Push him back down the beach.
Push him into the sea.
Push him across the waves.
Push him back into the boat.
Push the water out of his lungs.
Push him into his mother's arms.
Push the boat into another world,
where someone nice
gives him a fluffy toy
and a hot cup of cocoa
and says "*Welcome.*"
Push back the wet dark hair
to see him smile.
Push them all out of your mind.

Jacci Bulman

Khanh*

He points to who hasn't had a biscuit yet;
squats in the yard to watch other kids playing football;
watches us all.

He can't walk or talk,
sing or dance,
but somehow looks like he could do all of these
and more,
or none of it and still laugh.

What I see in him,
like the big answer on a rice grain,
is forgiveness.

He has somehow forgiven
God, the world, his country, his family,
the workers who treat him
like cheap meat,
tourists like me
who try to make him their souvenir,
forgiven us all,
and for that

he has gained something
I can't get into focus,
but it is grace.

*Khanh inspired us to name The Kianh Foundation in his honour B
a charity for children with disabilities in Vietnam, www.kianh.org.uk*

Sarah Doyle

Unholy

Is this a holy thing to see?
Our leaders state it's not our war –
it's just another refugee
washed up on yet another shore.

The politicians close their ears
to drowning children's desperate cries;
build barriers to guard frontiers
against the swarms who'd colonise.

No safety, homes or livelihoods,
they seek a respite from attack.
Displaced, disowned, no worldly goods;
the hand of friendship knocks them back.

Oh, where is kindness? Where is hope?
Are we so poor, we will not share?
Rich nations claim they cannot cope –
they mean it's prudent not to care.

The message shouted, loud and clear:
stay on your foreign boats and rot.
A life is cheap, but aid is dear.
Our country's full. The sea is not.

Margaret Ives

Bergen-Belsen

The birch-tree forest here is beautiful,
But no birds sing.
The grass is green with Springtime radiance,
But grows in silence.
The rain falls softly from the skies
Into the stillness.

There are some gravestones here,
But those whose names are written on them
Do not lie there.
The liberators, when they came,
Kept no records.
They just cleared the mound of corpses
Into the gaping wounds
Dug in the grieving earth.

But sometimes you may see
Small groups of people
Stop by those gravestones
And pray together,
Seeking closure.

Danny Rivers

On Golden Beach

The duteous policeman stooped to lift you,
cradled you away from the sated sea on up
the stony, stillborn beach.
Anonymous no more, yet only your name
reached these shores. I want to know,
Did you spy the lights of a promised land?
Did they lilt and twinkle? Did you call out?
Did you shout to your brother in a flash of delight,
before your hand slipped his clasp,
your arms were flails,
and the crashing spray
punched your breath away?

Ambrose Musiyiwa

The Man Who Ran Through the Tunnel

When I heard
how he ran
across continents
over rivers
through forests
through deserts
and through tunnels,
how could I fail
to be inspired?

Paul McGrane

Workhouse

*Old tarry rope was painstakingly unravelled in workhouses to make oakum --
used in shipbuilding for packing the joints of timbers.*

I earn a little money but mainly
I'm paid in blisters and a broken back
and there's nothing I can do about it.
They needed a way to plug every hole
in the wooden ships of the Royal Fleet
without it costing an arm and a leg
and guess who they found to trick out that thread
from old bits of rope as fat as a noose?
To ask for more would be a big mistake
and my rations could be cut for a week.
What I choose to say is nothing at all.

I'm allowed in the garden, now and then,
where today the sky is coated in tar
and rain slicks through a crack in the gutter.
I suck in lung-smoke as a medicine.
A blackbird has been picking on a worm.
His life must be repetition like mine,
from birdsong on the kitchen roof at dawn
to roosting in the apple tree at dusk,
but one thing he has I may never have
and I want to pull at every feather,
remove his possibility of flight.

John Christopher Brown

Steep Stones, Small Steps

Carefully shaped, wood that fit
Because he followed its natural bent
The way he never once worried about a level yard
Knowing that years of conversation
Between foot, ground and weather would
Bring it to its own completion, allow it to
Take the shape his family's endurance allowed.

His tools, the handles of his shovels, his axes, his plows
Achieved forms less imposed than paid attention to,
As he helped them to come into their own.
Nothing straight might ever have been made
From the twisted wood his apple trees gave
But the preachers had gotten it wrong
For wood, like kids, can find a shape that fits them
If you pay enough attention to their natural grain.
Anyway. That's what my Grandfather believed.

I have found the separate pieces of his beehive,
The one my father had for so long set aside.
I don't know if I can find my way to rebuilding it
But I can't not try, not now. If only because we three
Were and are who we became, and because
There is yet wood enough in the world and my
Grandfather's tools to hand.

Ambrose Musiyiwa

Martians. Effing Martians

Shall we blame Martians
for everything that is wrong
with the world?
Shall we scan every building
every meeting
living
breathing
space
for signs of Martians?
Shall we prod Earthlings
ask them to be on guard
and report
round up
or bash
any Martian
sighted
or imagined?
Shall we bring out the spaceships
and start patrolling the streets?
Shall we fit PA systems to the spaceships
and play messages on a loop
telling Martians to go back home
that if they do not leave voluntarily
we will come for them
and forcibly remove them?
Shall we round up all Martians
put them in detention centres
put them on the next spaceship to Mars?
Shall we gas them?
Shall we nuke them?

Charlie Lambert

Statue of Liberty

Woke up this morning
Looked out to sea
No huddled masses!
Strange. New to me.

Checked the torch
Did freedom still glow?
No, flame's got a problem
But what? I don't know.

Trying to fix it
Get back on track
But someone keeps meddling
Behind my back.

Angela Locke

After the sky burial: Tibet

Red earth still clings to you,
left behind after the sky burial,
the ritual burning of clothes.
I was the first to touch you, melted down
from coin silver, a sliver of a life;
memories of my father, one of the last
to give his body willingly to the vultures,
this block twice melted in the fire.
He meant to leave, fleeing through mountains,
over the pass with his yaks,
but his heart never made the journey.
Perhaps the vultures will carry his soul
beyond the Napso La, into freedom.
This gift from his homeland, freely given,
left lying in the ashes of his clothes;
the twice-burned calendar which marked his life,
I will bring with me into exile.

Dick Jones

Leon Greenman 1910 - 2008

I am called survivor, one who has
come through fog then fire to stand
before you here. I am an
ordinary man on a journey

through the dark. And my life
is a commodity: I give you, out
of a dream, my wife, my child,
the vapour they became;

this number etched in midnight
blue inside my arm; the names
that I, the cantor, sing in place
of the Kaddish – Westerbork and

Birkenau, Monowitz and
Buchenwald; the smoke that
rising effaces a winter sun.
I float my memories on

the still air, watch a small, bleak
wisdom rise behind your eyes.
These are the words: when I'm gone,
bear this for me. Never forget.

Dick Jones

Migrants

Each night before I go to bed I check the kids.
And because they lie so still – an arm across a throat,
a cruciform, half in, half out, a starfish beached –

I have to lean across to find a shadow pulse, a rising
diaphragm, a hair that floats on an outbound breath.
I have to do this, but I know, of course, that it's only

in their dreams they're out at sea. And that
it's only this night's tide and the sleep it brings
in which they seem to drown.

Jennifer Johnson

Remembering Srebrenica

Many, like me, remember Srebrenica
as the sickening horror on TV
that went with *ethnic cleansing*,
a *safe haven* that proved unsafe.

Fewer know that Srebrenica
translates as silver mine,
remember the dangerous darkness
from which its currency's extracted,

how the fury of underground fires
caused explosions, roof falls,
hardened edge-defining difference
grief's exit could not soften.

Sandra Horn

The day peace came

Some claimed it was foreseen, foretold
In Tarot cards, in holy writ, in portents –
The blossoming of a sacred tree,
A halo round the moon,
A rainbow in a cloudless sky.
Who knows? It came so suddenly, in silence;
The silence of no guns, no bombs,
No shouts, no screaming.
No-one slapped a child,
Wielded a jack-knife, swore,
Strangled, kicked, mugged, raped.
But what were we to do? What now?
We wept, at first.
We wept, and could not meet each others' eyes.
How to begin again? Anew? We did not know.

Then the first hand reached out...

Stephanie Green

Give me your Hand

[Inspired by 'Give me your Hand' Tabhair dom do Lámh (Irish Gaelic) by the blind harpist Ruaidrí Dáll Ó'Catháin (c 1570-c.1650).]

Touch finger tip to finger tip:
thumbs, index to index,
tall man to tall man,
ring to ring, pinkie to pinkie.

Take this invisible gift
in the cradle of your hands;
shield it, as it flickers in the draught
of all our cold, dreich days.

Here is a word without vowel or consonant.
It is a language you have never heard before
but understand immediately.

Jack Houston

Allinthistogether

We're squeezed into   the corners
cups of tea perched   on knees
while they   take up

        the middle
        of the room
        as if they own
        the place.

polite   we sigh
and blow   to cool our drinks.

They flap
        ears &
      the breeze
    created lifts
the air.

We try   to make the best
of awkwardness, pointedly
not noticing   defecations
nor their stampings of feet.

But our   attempts
at conversation   falter

      as through
     their tree-trunk
    legs we can't see
      eye to eye.

     One of them
    trumpets loud
    and lowers
     a trunk
to slurp at your tea.

You force   a smile
& turn toward the window.

The day outside is bright & clear & free.

John Gohorry

You sit on the back row

*No-one made a greater mistake than he who did
nothing because he could only do a little.*
                              - *Edmund Burke*

You sit on the back row
watching the action unravel
- a child at a border fence
blinded by tear gas,
a dictator, ninety-odd now, partying on
in his drought-ridden dictatorship,
the seismic aftershocks
of an underground atomic explosion,
a massacre in a high school,
starvation, rapes, torture, beheadings.

On stage, public speaking
is an art of deception,
the candidates in the roadshow
building walls with their rhetoric,
and party smears all that's on offer
to purge our dystopias.

The Senecan pageant rolls on,
its bloodthirsty improvisations
remorseless as clockwork;
the roadshow antagonists deliver
the lines they have learned by heart.

It must all run its course, you think,
nothing can change it now.

Except you, in the darkness,
free to stay, free to leave,
can exercise freedom of thought,
and now the lights come on

leave your seat on the back row,
walk out onto the street, into
the rest of your life and there,
resolute in the hurl of traffic,
make what difference you can.

Clare Crossman

Fine Foods est. 1954

I remember Mr Perowicz's shadowed
delicatessen, the sausages wrapped in paper
and cut by hand.
Tomatoes, onions, gherkins
in vinegar, as if summer was kept in jars.
He'd put the shelves in necessary order.

Neat in his white overall, he kept his counsel
and never said how he'd arrived,
or why he'd fled.
It was personal to him, his walk
to work through our provincial town
a freedom, or a journey of forgetting.

It was his wife who negotiated
belonging. In sentences of night class
grammar, she spoke when she took
the money. I stuttered 'schleb'
when I asked for bread.

I loved the cool difference of their shop,
the smell of cabbage and cheese,
as if it was a slice of earth.
A gate to lean on in their country,
the names in unpronounceable script,
a somewhere else of marbled surfaces,
  light held immaculate in glass.

That was our exchange,
what they had always known
and what was new to me; an exile
made of Pomeranian salt, amber,
and herring-silver. Another place
rich and harsh, as the slate grey
distance from the Baltic sea.

Kathleen Jones

The Year Zero

It was the year there was no summer
when winter drizzled and froze
through a reluctant spring
into a cloud-shrouded August
snowdrops in April and
February Fill-dyke in July.
We had no name for these new seasons
or the year that refused to turn
in its old rhythms.

It was the year that our mythologies lost
meaning and the oracles were dumb.
Hawberries glutted the warm winter
red skies at night brought only storm.
We had no signs to warn us of the plague-
beetle in the bark, no animal or bird
to augur the weirding weather –
geese stopped migrating and
the swallows stayed.

It was the year we found that we no longer
spoke the language of the land. The year
science had no answer to the big question.
The year we knew we needed a new story
to tell us how to live.

Sarah Mnatzaganian

Morning

To Elisabeth

I had a Gretel moment back there
until I spotted yellow poplar leaves spattering the path
and knew I had seen them before,

surprised by their bright circles against the mud
on my way through fine rain
early this late-August morning.

Nearly home, I find a congregation of trees
at the head of the valley. They have no book;
they are here to breathe, drink light and listen.

From time to time, a motherly dove or a dark rook speaks.
Wind sends quiet applause through the leaves of oak and ash
and the sun bowls light straight down the valley.

I would give this morning to those I do not even love,
whom I have never met,
who are not yet born.

Steph Morris

FAQs of Gardens

Are they really in keeping,
these foreign plants,
palms and tree ferns?

                You're not asking us
                to dig them up
                now their roots are in deep,
                now they're intertwined?
                Do you think belonging
                means sameness?
                Who says what fits where?
                Get with the new ecology.

Do they really like it here?

                You can't see them,
                sprouting and blooming,
                fronds frolicking
                through the flat-leaved trees?
                Contributing carbon
                for all they're worth?

Can we provide for
their cultural needs?

                These plants
                will sort themselves out.
                They have the conditions
                they need.
                Can you provide for yours?
                Do you even know
                what they are?

Dasylirion? Have I said
the name right?

                No. Make an effort.
                You can say dandelion alright.

Were they sown round here?

                                      A lot of them, yes.
                                      Some in Holland.
                                      Some in the opposite
                                      hemisphere.
                                      Does it matter?

What do you mean it was
all just swamps here once?

                                      Why do you think
                                      the streets have names
                                      like Lower Marsh?
                                      It was bogs from here
                                      to Croydon,
                                      no Victorian terraces,
                                      or London planes,
                                      which are the hybrid offspring
                                      of immigrants, by the way.

Aren't they taking over?

                                      So what if they are?
                                      Deal with it.

Is there any space left?

                                      Yes.

Martyn Halsall

Kavanagh's Field

To know fully one field or one land is a lifetime's experience. In the world of poetic experience it is depth that counts, not width.
PJ Kavanagh: *The Parish and the Universe.* (1967)

Wandering through words I encounter PJ Kavanagh
in his approximate hat, a patched coat as I remember,
leaning on a gate, watching the same deep field
he had always known, as if waiting for it to harvest.

I turned the page, but if I'd had time to pause
I'd have asked him about detail, and fascination;
what caused him to pause: the list of a stone wall,
exchange of tenanted sheep and cattle, angle

of a lone hawthorn sculpted to a banner by sea wind;
and offered him in exchange one field I recall
from walking it a thousand times with a collie:
its angle leaned against sky, its limestone rib

exposed through a wound in the grazing, its stand of beech
running like a ripple in current, its rise and roll
of runrigs, like barrow mounds, tidal depths of grass
as seasons passed through, following light and waymark.

I imagine if I turned back the page again
Kavanagh would be there still; the familiar ash plant
propped up against his shadow. I could offer him
also a walk by the river, and water's riot

over the old weir, raised after a dry October,
and the channel that led to the wheel, and how the mill
is now rented to those affording luxury.
I doubt he would follow that line, after a shrug,

preferring to wait for what was news on his ground,
rehearsing the familiar, and finding it always new:
that sudden gust that parted the long-edged grass,
that answering owl, echo to his hands' cupped summons;

preferring to stay outside while his wireless set
recited the six o'clock tragedies of that evening:
his headline how he watched the forest fire of a fox,
and read night off the manuscript of star-gazing.

Katherine Gallagher

The Year of the Tree

I carried a tree
through the Underground.

It was hard. At first,
people scarcely noticed me

and the oak I was lugging
along the platforms –

heavier than a suitcase
and difficult to balance.

We threaded through corridors,
changing lines: up and down stairs,

escalators, and for a moment
I imagined everyone on the planet

taking turns
to carry a tree as daily rite.

A few people asked
Why a tree?

I said it was for my own
edification –

a tree always
has something to teach.

***

Sharp gusts
whirred through the corridors

rustling the branches
as I hurried on

past the sweepers
picking up rubbish, scraps of paper.

*Be sure to take the tree
with you*, they said.

*Don't worry, I'm taking it
to my garden,*

the start of a forest.
When people stared,

Relax, I said,
it's a tree, not a gun.

Sarala Estruch

If

If you knew what it is to foster life
in the depths of your body,
to be the grass stalk, clasping
its progeny, that drinks to satiation
then roots further in. If you knew
what it is to be the rose bush
that grows thorns in order to protect its buds
or the amaryllis that lies dormant
for months, gathering strength,
to bring forth the shoot
with its oval bud. If you knew
what it is to be the bud
that bursts into flower, petals
unfolding in an orgy of colour
or the tree that watches its blossoms fall
at the end of a season
only to return the following spring
with a fresh bouquet, ready to give.
If you were present – in full flesh
and full heart – when dawn shines
on green life, then you would hold
each seed in the palm of your hand
and raise it up to the light.

Carol Caffrey

Post-partum

Night cloaks all living things
and earth itself holds its breath;
wildfires flicker here and there
while other patches
of the wasted land shrivel
under smoke and ash.
When day exhales at last a snapping twig,
a rustle in the windless trees, brings suspicion not relief.

We are in the debatable lands now,
no longer speak in the easy ways.
Within the borders of silence
we take a breath, take someone's
measure before we ask:
which way did you vote, then?

Alison Luterman

What We Did In the Resistance (Part 1)

In the beginning, we wept.
Well, some of us wept.
Some of us walked around stunned
as if pieces of sky
had fallen out of the sky and revealed themselves
to be chunks of blue plaster.
We examined the chunks.
We shook plaster dust out of our hair--there was so much dust!
We craned our necks and stared up.
Now we saw the scaffolding,
the what-do-you-call-it--sheetrock?
The drywall, the lath. We saw the insulation,
full of asbestos, we saw how the walls were stuffed
with it, like money. Everything
was revealed, yet nothing was clear.
If we were in a cunningly-devised structure
not of our making, was it a theater
or a prison, a shopping mall or a mausoleum?

In the beginning, as I have said, we wept.
We embraced on the street when we saw each other.
We sat in cafes drinking coffee, digesting our grief.
The rest of the time we sat in front of glowing screens.
We gathered at night and made signs:
Not My President and Pussy Grabs Back;
we stapled them to sticks
and marched in exultation all over the world.
We had never seen before how many of us there are.

We clicked and liked and signed and donated and called
our Congresspeople, and sent postcards and checks.
We spoke of girding ourselves for the long fight.
We spoke of a marathon, we spoke of walking
in the footsteps of the elders, we spoke
of coal miners in Pennsylvania and Kentucky

who had voted for Trump.

And still the cat box needed to be cleaned, the oil in the car changed,
classes taught, bills paid, dishes washed.
And still the rains came down, epically, biblically--
we joked about End Times--and the witching trees
with their bare black branches sprouted the tiniest of new buds,
almost invisible at first, a red tip at the nodes, a subtle fire,
and then overnight, purple blossoms.
Trees who know nothing of elections, who preach only
the gospel of persistence. For,
despite everything, earth continued to turn
from light to darkness and into light again,
over and over it rolled,
as it had been rolling through generations of empire and uprising,
extinction and evolution, and once again
to our surprise we noticed that it was Spring.

Christine Vial

Vial Girl

A *Vial: a small container, usually of glass, for holding liquids.*
As a surname, most commonly associated with France or French ancestry.
Dictionary of surnames.

All my life my surname has been anglicised, mispronounced,
 mangled , mocked.
Endlessly I explain, tell the tale of the Huguenot silk weavers
who originally fled to Spitalfields in London's East -End from
 France in 1572
to escape the massacre of St Bartholomew's Eve and then again, in
 1681,
when Charles II offered sanctuary from on-going persecution.

My father, growing up in Brick Lane, poor and politicised, in the
 1930's Depression,
was a tool-maker, not a silk weaver, and knew nothing of his ancestry :
all he had were the assumptions made locally when you have a
 French surname.
He gave me that French surname, his radical politics and the DNA
 of survival.

The rich and the rooted have family trees. The poor, the migrants,
 the dispossessed,
 have a scorched-earth history; might have nothing but words,
languages lost over time, family names, to chart their lineage.

I have no paper proof but this is my heritage.
Now I am proud to name it and claim it.

Kelly Davis

Georgian box, Tullie House Museum, Carlisle

The grey lead octagon has traces
of red paint on its sides.
What story could those stains tell?
Were the box open now,
would I smell
200-year-old tobacco?

Every day, a hand reached out
in a sunlit Georgian parlour,
opened this box,
and plundered
its twisted golden store
to fill a long-stemmed pipe.

The lid is topped with an African head.
The face is tilted upwards
so a thumb can cover mouth and nose,
gripping just under the chin,
pulling up, and up,
until the last breath goes…

Lynda Turbet

Spilled Water*

Barefoot on stones,
skinny goat-legs dust grey
she stoops to the river's sluggish flow,
to balance on her head
a dream of gleaming taps,
water gushing free
a crisp white uniform.
Rain.

She could not count the men.
How long might she stand
beneath an icy waterfall
lashed by its cleansing torrent?
She could not count the years.

Old hands like claws; a blade's glint;
blood floods; the pain
a fire no water can put out.
Without this – shame.
School? We'll teach her:
a bullet to the brain.

Girl, I would gather you
in cupped hands unspilled
carry you to a warm rockpool
make your precious drops a sea
and watch the tide.

* *A Chinese expression for a female baby*

Ceinwen Haydon

No Woman is Indispensable

my daughter　　　　　　　　*today the executive order was made*
your belly swells
I wanted this so much
a grandchild
continuation of love
how can I comfort you
you carry a girl　　　　　　*girl children will be given up*

　　　　　　　　　　　　　　to the appetites of masters
　　　　　　　　　　　　　　to the needs of masters
　　　　　　　　　　　　　　to satisfy masters
when they fade
they will be discarded　　　　*in unmarked places*

and replaced by fresh rosebuds

Elizabeth Stott

I Grow My Hair

I grow my hair until it is a wide spread
of eagle wings. And you run afraid, as a rabbit runs
before the dark shape on the ground.
You raise a small cloud of dust.
I raise you to the sun.

I grow my hair until it is a wide sweep
of ocean. You sail my storms in fear; steer
by the stars and sun until I suck your ship
into my deep currents. Our atoms become one.
We are rain, grass, rabbits.

I grow my hair until it is a wide curl
of light from a supernova. It envelops planets,
tangles the universe. I drag you, screaming, to
oblivion, yet you are made from the dust of stars.
You dream of them.

I grow my hair until it is a wide lick
of a tongue that speaks things men fear more than death.
If you would escape this, then run, my darling, run.
You raise a small cloud of dust.
I raise you to the sun.

Elizabeth Stott

Reconstruction

My friend wishes to re-make herself from sackcloth and ashes.

Take the ashes of stars, I advise,
and sackcloth made
from the recycled garments of saints.

You haven't seen the scars, she replies.

Months later, after doing nothing,
she decides on brown paper and string.

I tell her that she must use brown paper shaved
from the sunlight that skims fields of ripe grain at harvest –
string twisted from the hair of mermaids.

She tells me I should reconsider the blonde streaks, go on a diet.

For a year, her clothes make her look like a parcel,
covering her from shoulder to knee.

I am so lucky, I know. I carry on with my sympathy,
stop wearing low-cut blouses in her company.

Abruptly, she moves on.

Her wrapping is gone, leaving a soft, pale form.
She says that sand and straw will do to pad her out.

Then take the sand from eternity's hourglass I tell her,
and the straw from the stable of a unicorn.

Apparently, I am fatuous, and probably vain.
I go away – reconsider the blonde streaks, go on a diet.

In my absence, she fashions for herself a golden bodice,
more beautiful than the breastplate of a queen's battledress.

She tells me that one must earn this.

Harriet Fraser

a sort of hypnosis

It was a gentle intent.
I would, I was told, tap into early memories
stored as sure as sinews and bones,
discover imprints, origins of my habits,
loves and fears.

Back I went. I saw myself: girl, child, baby.
And then, all went dark. I teetered on the edge
of lives and time before me

and then I fell. A thick darkness,
a fire, flames, the arms of women,
blooded hands, slender wrists of girls
abused. My eyes met eyes, hundreds of eyes.
Hollowed out stares of submission
faces streaked with tears and all the air
was wailing, cries of loss, the agony of rape
and afterwards a quiet, the dull despair
that spreads like ink on cloth.

I curled into a ball
tight as a stone
heavy as this history.

I don't know how much time passed
I felt a wakening, a swell, a rage stoked
by whispers, then by shouts, women
marching, heads held high
powered by a repeated

No!

It was as if all the women
who had cried and cowered
and fought rose up as one.

And with this rising
I uncurled, and stood,
raised my head, released
the voice of a tribe, roaring.

Clare Shaw

Are we there yet?

There's a woman in Kabul who's saying *No*
but in Bolton a woman is feeling – first time in years –
the air on her face like clean water.
She doesn't know it yet
but in months she'll say *Almost*. We're almost there.

And of course, there's always my daughter,
shouting *I want to run* and looking for birds and the moon
but a twenty-two year old in Nottingham
cannot wear her own shoes,
and a woman west of Glasgow is planning her death

in seventeen days come-what-may.
and that's not, of course, allowing for
the thirty-five women on one street in Luton
who say *Yes*
because they don't have any choice,

or how long this journey has taken, the exhaustion -
and the sense that someone else is in control
and so many have no money for a ticket
or have not even left home yet,
thinking that nowhere is better.

Somewhere, someone believes in a 'there'
where we all want to be together,
where hurts are mended
and daylight and rain are in perfect proportion
and our children are in our arms

and will never be taken
or fall.
There, where the answer is *Yes*,
where day breaks open with a great, bright "YES"
spoken over and over to the sky.

I want to believe, to know that
we're not running for the sake of it,
or away from some horror -
a child face down in the water,
our houses ransacked in our sleep.

So listen – wherever we're heading,
I'm in. With three (very simple) provisions:

this time, nobody gets hurt

or missed out. And
no-one is left behind.

Mary Powell

A Weight of Words

Pray be quiet. *(Shut Up)*
Your too many words usurp
my small pages. Most fall
off the edge. I am losing
hours and hours, whole days
trying to get it.

Your discretionary devils
close my thoughts in boxes
line them, one row upon
another, ready to be shot at.

When you cut me
from my mother
tongue, it bled into this soil
that's not the soil I belong in.
There's so much of it,
in my mouth.

In my ears, your drums
beat so fast, I cannot jump
to them anymore.
Shush! Listen.

I am not who I was
when the steel
– capped boots marched
upon my breast,
squeezed out the milk
flattened every scar
of love and hate
made of me a stain.

Please do not wrap me
in that stole, spun

by another girl's mother,
for I will not be at her behest.

Instead, cast me once more
upon the waters
for mercy's sake.
Let me not be diminished
for your child, in time
may have need
of a Pharoah or her daughter.

Nicola Jackson

Our Girls

The radio alarm this morning
leaked a slow dark stain.
Some deaths are quick
and almost fine.
These have caused the stars
to reel in pain.

Take my morning cup
of Earl Grey tea.
Take the slow swell of quiet sun
through the autumn glass.
Take the polished surface
of the bed-side chest,
my fingernails, my very skin.

Listen
to the echoes of their mother,
still speaking of the day that Daesh came.
Forced her to watch.

I look out of the window
and watch bleached leaves fall,

one by one.

Joan Michelson

Great Aunt Hero

Great Aunt Hero, whom we never met,
was a rebel and a bundle of lost
letters rumoured to be wonder-epics.

She travelled from Boston, Massachusetts
to San Francisco, to the wilds of China,
to Moscow, Dresden, Honolulu and Oahu.

On Oahu she married a Catholic native,
although she had been born a Jew,
which her six children never knew;

nor the story of her abrupt departure:
thrown out by her father (who loved her)
for a misdemeanour with a Harvard suitor.

This happened about the time she bobbed her hair,
sent her mother to night school, and heady
with the news of Bolshevik success, joined

the Party, which she subsequently left.
A picture shows her with her family orchestra.
She's on a bench, in black performance dress

standing with her baton raised and pointed high.
I feel her power in the distance and I see her
rise, explosive as a rare supernova.

Making waves, she begets new stars.

Pippa Little

How Helen Steven, Activist, Scratched An Adrienne Rich Poem On Her Cell Door in Dumbarton Police Station, Scotland

A cell's got nothing but time in it
and a night that never grows dark.

You sit on the slab and stare at the door,
slammed from outside by a warder

who wouldn't meet your eye.
The door's scratched Pictish snarls,

first names, gang names, sex-oaths and enemies
force you to focus. But by 2 a.m.

you can't rewrite these broke-back alphabets,
need to leave more for the next woman and the next –

words itch your palms, you
look about for some instrument –

keys taken, but you've got your jeans
so you step out of them for the zip's

metal tag and make a start;
hours it takes, most of the night, fingers

sting from the carving, but near to morning it's
complete, as much embedded in the wood

as the poet's concentrated gaze
all the while, white-hot upon your back.

Elizabeth Hare

At the '100 women' conference at the BBC in October 2013 Zainab Bangura, the delegate from Sierra Leone, spoke about Malala and said that if a young girl was ever again shot for trying to go to school all the women in the world should take to the streets.

If Only

It is the schoolgirls who come out first
Angry, tearful, running across playgrounds
Leaving their books and their jotters open
Their teachers follow them, and together
Shouting they take to the streets

The old women hear them, see them from their windows
And come out in wheelchairs and walking frames
They leave their firesides and their daytime TV
Leave their bingo and their drawing classes
Leave their kitchens and gardens, their afternoon naps
Their pensioners' lunches and their reading groups
With the children they take to the streets

By now the word has got round and the whole world knows
Women leave sewing machines idle in Shanghai sweatshops
Buckets half filled at wells in India, rugs unwoven in Egypt
They leave the beaches in Australia and Argentina
They leave the brothels in Thailand and Saigon
They leave health centres and care homes and nurseries
Hair salons and hotel receptions
They leave parliamentary committees and research labs
Law courts, surgeries and consulting rooms
They leave studios and drawing boards
Rehearsals, lecture theatres and boardrooms
Together they take to the streets

Then the mothers and housewives come
Leaving floors un-mopped, phones unanswered
Dinners uncooked, washing un-hung

Trolleys abandoned in the aisles of supermarkets
Children unfed and husbands unnerved

When half the world has taken to the streets
The world itself falls silent, waiting
And the man
Who was going to shoot the little girl on her way to school
Puts down his gun
And walks away

Nicola Jackson

My Wall

I am planning on building a wall.
I am contemplating this wall.
I do not know where it will go,
nor where it will trace its way.

I think my wall will be beautiful,
pale flowers will drift across the stone.
Creepers will trail soft tendrils,
their downy- backed leaves like hands

reaching out on both sides of my wall.
Birds will nest in the tangle of new growth.
They will sing in that tentative way
birds have as they emerge in Spring.

There will be many gates. None
will be locked. There will be no Arbeit arch.
It will be understood that each is free,
that each gate always will stand open.

My wall will have kind custodians
to tend tired travellers as they arrive.
Like Mediaeval monks, they will wash feet,
bathe hands, make up simple truckle beds.

Each family can stay together, take time
for the very old to live, to pass away
while the birds are singing. We can all
mourn by our accepted practices.

There will be many grassy places
for the children to play together.
And this is what will protect us.

Catherine Graham

Sticks and Stones

Even though you beat me,
you cannot keep me under your table.

You beat me
to put me in my right place
as a woman. My right place is being free.

Free to fight for the right to speak out.
Speak out against injustice, inaction, poverty.

If you believe that pain will
make me put my hands over my mouth,
then you are misled.

I cup my hands up to my lips and drink
to Justice, Equality, Dignity.

For I do not fade like a bruise fades,
I heal like a broken bone.

Alison Barr

We Are Clay

Timeworn towers speak across millennia
from Cumbria to Mesopotamia.
Hands scooped clay by Solway reed beds
and dug between the Tigris and Euphrates.
The Tower of Babel searched high for God.
By now He may have regretted forming
the shape of man in the Garden of Eden.

At the Empire's edge, Hadrian's Wall
and the river Eden, Itouna of rushing water,
yielded to a silver sea expanse.
Craftsmen pressed stamps into wet tiles,
preserving legions, emperors, the Empire.
Waxen masks peeled from the dead
stared blankly from wall niches.

Come let us make bricks and bake
them thoroughly. King James Bible.
Shape, stack, dry, kiln, fire, build.
Clay mingles with cobalt and sand.
Classic colours; Cumbrian Red, Fletton,
Staffordshire Blues, Accrington Bloods,
Silver Oxfordshire, London Browns.

Crumbling, powdery, smoothed, flecked.
Crevices are crammed with particles;
root, mineral, animal, shell, fish, petals.
Carboniferous atoms interconnect.
Sediment crushed, weathered, layered.
Water gushes over mountains, eroding
feldspar, mother of clay.

Existence over, men are laid to rest
under a thin skin earth, equal with the clay.
Castles and churches, rise, fall, crumble.

Border lines and walls shift with dark tides;
Hadrian's, Berlin, Jericho, Troy. And more.
Walls designed by minds echo barriers within.

Jacci Bulman

Dancing in Banjul

One month.
The banana-skin man has been
swirling each night around the compound,
to scare away evil.

One month.
The young girls of the family have been
kept in a room, legs bound,
to heal hurt flesh.

One month,
since the wise elder women said to
cut the girls, keep
in line with tradition.

And now the girls are coming out,
clean and cut nice,
so we all celebrate tonight
with a big dance

girls who can marry,
bring no shame on the family,
do what is said to be
religion,

and the banana-skin man
can stay home,
no evil to scare away,
all done.

Chaucer Cameron

Praise Be to Unexpected Ways

After Sepideh Jodeyri*

I have breasts, which I love, I can speak the word breast, I can write
    the word breast,
I can associate the breast with a robin on a branch. I love birds, I
love the way they sing, and how they capture territory in unexpected
    ways. Praise the breast.

I have lips, which I love, I can own the word lips, I can use my lips
    in unexpected ways.
I can slip my tongue through lips; associate the rhyme with pips
    from fruit,
hip from 1960's, hips that support the weight of a body.

I have a body, which I love, I love the word body, I love the way it lives,
in unexpected ways, comes back in dreams, the way it sneaks across
    the borders,
the way it joins with tongue, lips, breast, small birds on branches.
    Praise the body,
lips and breast, praise the tongue that can speak the censored word.

*Sepideh Jodeyri is an Iranian poet living in exile in Europe in order to keep writing poetry without censorship.

Paul McGrane

Welcome to my Country

Dear prospective citizen
thank you for your application

a State response will soon be sent
but here's mine:

I hope this soil will not for long
be foreign to your feet

that my weather
will be your weather

that my cities will offer their freedom
my countryside the right to roam

I'll be standing in Arrivals
with your name.